Wood Pellet

Smoker and Grill

Cookbook

The Complete Guide to Enjoy your Wood Pellet
Grill with Original Recipes Plus Secret Hacks and
Tricks to Take your BBQ to Upgrade

Kevin Parker

Disclaimer Notice:

Please note the information contained within this document is for educational and entertainment purposes only. All effort has been executed to present accurate, up to date, and reliable, complete information. No warranties of any kind are declared or implied. Readers acknowledge that the author is not engaging in the rendering of legal, financial, medical or professional advice. The content within this book has been derived from various sources. Please consult a licensed professional before attempting any techniques outlined in this book.

By reading this document, the reader agrees that under no circumstances is the author responsible for any losses, direct or indirect, which are incurred as a result of the use of information contained within this document, including, but not limited to, errors, omissions, or inaccuracies.

Table of Content

Introduction

Thank you for purchasing **Wood Pellet Smoker and Grill Cookbook: The Complete Guide to Enjoy your Wood Pellet Grill with Original Recipes Plus Secret Hacks and Tricks to Take your BBQ to Upgrade**

This culinary technique is nothing else than the evolution of a primitive need of cavemen who realized, despite themselves, that eating dead or killed animals without cooking the meat could be even lethal.

These people were the first ones to cook meat, fish and roots on the fire, experimenting, trying and understanding that by cooking they could obtain a better taste and a more digestible food, in fact this kind of cooking has arrived with some little devices up to now, given by evolution and technology.

Chicken & Beef Recipes

Traeger Asian Miso Chicken wings

Preparation Time: 15 minutes

Cooking Time: 25 minutes

Servings: 6

Ingredients:

- 2 lb. chicken wings

- ¾ cup soy

- ½ cup pineapple juice

- 1 tbsp. sriracha

- ⅛ cup miso

- ⅛ cup gochujang

- ½ cup water

- ½ cup oil

- Togarashi

Directions:

1.   Preheat the Traeger to 375°F

2.   Combine all the ingredients except togarashi in a Ziploc bag. Toss until the chicken wings are well coated. Refrigerate for 12 hours Pace the wings on the grill grates and close the lid. Cook for 25 minutes or until the internal temperature reaches

165°F Remove the wings from the Traeger and sprinkle Togarashi.

Nutrition:Calories: 703, Fat: 56g, Protein: 27g, Fiber: 1g, Sodium: 1156mg

Chicken Wings in Traegers

Preparation Time: 10 minutes

Cooking Time: 50 minutes

Servings: 1

Ingredients:

- 6–8 lbs. Chicken wings

- 1/3 cup Canola oil

- 1 tbsp. Barbeque seasoning mix

Directions:

1. Combine the seasonings and oil in one large bowl.

2. Put the chicken wings in the bowl and mix well.

3. Turn your traeger to the 'smoke' setting and leave it on for 4–5 minutes.

4. Set the heat to 350°F and leave it to preheat for 15 minutes with the lid closed.

5. Place the wings on the grill with enough space between the pieces.

6. Let it cook for 45 minutes or until the skin looks crispy.

7. Remove from the grill and serve with your choice of sides.

Nutrition:

- Protein: 33 g

- Fat: 8 g

- Sodium: 134 mg

- Cholesterol: 141 mg

Smoked Beef Churl Barbecue

Preparation Time: 20 minutes

Cooking Time: 4 hours

Servings: 10

Ingredients:

- 1 5 pound-beef chuck rolls

- 5 tbsp. ground black peppercorns

- ¼ cup kosher salt

Directions:

1. Combine salt and black peppercorns in a bowl. Mix until combined.

2. Rub the beef chuck with the spice mixture then set aside.

3. Preheat a grill over medium heat for about 10 minutes.

4. Place the charcoal on the grill then waits until the grill reaches 275°F (135°C).

5. Wrap the beef with aluminum foil then place on the grill. Keep the grill's temperature to 275°F (135°C)

6. Cook the beef chuck for 5 hours.

7.   When the smoked beef is done, take the smoked beef out of the grill then let it cool for a few minutes.

8.   Cut the smoked beef into thin slices then serves with any kind of roasted vegetables, as you desired.

Nutrition:

- Calories: 230 Carbs: 22g Fat: 9g Protein: 15g

Herb Smoked Chicken

Preparation Time: 10 minutes

Cooking Time: 16 minutes

Servings: 6

Ingredients:

- 3 tbsp. olive oil
- 1 tsp. thyme
- 1 tsp. ground black pepper or to taste
- 4 tbsp. freshly squeezed lemon juice
- 1 tbsp. lemon zest
- 1 tbsp. freshly chopped parsley
- 1 tsp. salt or taste
- 1 tbsp. chopped rosemary
- 2 tbsp. freshly chopped cilantro
- 6 boneless chicken breasts

Directions:

1. In a large mixing bowl, combine the thyme, oil, pepper, juice, lemon zest, parsley, rosemary, cilantro and salt. Add the chicken breast and toss to combine. Cover the mixing bowl and refrigerate for 1 hour.

2.   Remove the chicken breast from the marinade and let it rest for a few minutes until it is at room temperature.

3.   Start your grill on smoke, leaving the lid opened for 5 minutes or until fire starts.

4.   Close the lid and preheat grill to 450°F with the lid closed for 10–15 minutes, using mesquite traegers.

5.   Arrange the chicken breasts onto the grill grate and smoke for 16 minutes, 8 minutes per side, or until the internal temperature of the chicken reaches 165°F.

6.   Remove the chicken breasts from the grill and let them rest for a few minutes.

7.   Serve and top with your favorite sauce.

Nutrition:

- Calories: 207
- Fat 11.2g
- Carbohydrate 1.2g
- Fiber: 0.5g
- Protein: 25.2g

Honey Glazed Smoked Beef

Preparation Time: 10 minutes Cooking Time: 8 hours

Servings: 10 Ingredients:

- 1 6-pound beef brisket

- 2 ½ tbsp. salt

- 2 ½ tbsp. pepper

- ¾ cup barbecue sauce

- 3 tbsp. red wine

- 3 tbsp. raw honey

Directions:

1. Preheat the smoker to 225°F (107°C). Spread the charcoal on one side.

2. Meanwhile, rub the beef brisket with salt, pepper, and barbecue sauce.

3. When the smoker has reached the desired temperature, place the brisket on the grill with the fat side up. Splash red wine over beef brisket.

4. Smoke the beef brisket for 8 hours. Check the smoker every 2 hours and add more charcoal if it is necessary.

5.   Once it is done, take the smoked beef brisket from the smoker then transfers it to a serving dish.

6.   Drizzle raw honey over the beef and let it sit for about an hour before slicing. Serve with roasted or sautéed vegetables according to your desire.

Nutrition: Calories: 90 Carbs: 8g Fat: 1g Protein: 11g Pork Recipes

Braised Pork Chile Verde

Preparation Time: 10 minutes

Cooking Time: 40 minutes

Servings: 6

Ingredients:

- 3 pounds' pork shoulder, bone removed and cut into ½ inch cubes

- 1 tbsp. all-purpose flour

- Salt and pepper to taste

- 1-pound tomatillos, husked and washed

- 2 jalapenos, chopped

- 1 medium yellow onion, peeled and cut into chunks

- 4 cloves garlic

- 4 tbsp. extra virgin olive oil

- 2 cup chicken stock

- 2 cans green chilies

- 1 tbsp. cumin

- 1 tbsp. oregano

- ½ lime, juiced

- ¼ cup cilantro

Directions:

1. Place the pork shoulder chunks in a bowl and toss with flour -season with salt and pepper to taste.

2. Use desired traeger when cooking. Place a large cast-iron skillet on the bottom rack of the grill. Close the lid and preheat for 15 minutes.

3. Place the tomatillos, jalapeno, onion, and garlic on a sheet tray lined with foil and drizzle with two tbsp. olive oil - season with salt and pepper to taste.

4. Place the remaining olive oil in the heated cast iron skillet and cook the pork shoulder. Spread the meat evenly, then close.

5. Before closing the lid, place the vegetables in the tray on the grill rack. Close the lid of the grill.

6. Cook for 20 minutes without opening the lid or stirring the pork. After 20 minutes, remove the vegetables from the grill and transfer to a blender. Pulse until smooth and pour into the pan with the pork. Stir in the chicken stock, green chilies, cumin, oregano, and lime juice—season with salt and

pepper to taste. Close the grill lid and cook for another 20 minutes. Once cooked, stir in the cilantro.

Nutrition:

- Calories: 389

- Protein: 28.5g

- Carbs: 4.5g

- Fat: 24.3g

- Sugar: 2.1g

BQ Pulled Pork Sandwiches

Preparation Time: 10 minutes

Cooking Time: 1 hour 30 minutes

Servings: 6

Ingredients:

- 8–10 lbs. bone-in pork butt roast

- 12 Kaiser Rolls

- 1 cup yellow mustard

- Coleslaw

- 1 bottle BBQ sauce

- 5 oz. Sugar

Directions

1. Push the temperature to 225°F and set your smoker to preheat

2. Now take out the pork roast from the packaging and keep it on a cookie sheet

3. Rub it thoroughly with yellow mustard

4. Now take a bowl and mix the BBQ sauce along with sugar in it

5. Use this mix to rub the roast thoroughly and give time for the rub to seep inside and melt in the meat

6. Now place this roast in the smoker and allow it to cook for 6 hours

7. When done, remove it from the smoker and

8. then wrap it in tin foil

9. Push the temperature to 250°F and cook it for a couple of hours. The internal temperature should reach 200°F

10. Let the pork butt rest in the foil for an hour before pulling it out

11. Now take the Kaiser roll and cut it in half

12. Mix the pulled pork with some BBQ sauce and pile on the top of each halved roll

13. Top it with coleslaw and serve

Nutrition:

- Calories: 426

- Protein: 65.3g

- Carbs: 20.4g

- Fat: 8.4g

- Sugar: 17.8g

Pork Belly Burnt Ends

Preparation Time: 30 minute Cooking Time: 6 hours

Servings: 8 to 10 Ingredients:

•   1 (3-pound) skinless pork belly (if not already skinned, use a sharp boning knife to remove the skin from the belly), cut into 1½- to 2-inch cube

•   1 batch Sweet Brown Sugar: Rub

•   ½ cup honey

•   1 cup Bill's Best BBQ Sauce

•   2 tbsp. light brown sugar

Directions:

1.   Supply your smoker with a traeger and follow the manufacturer's specific start-up procedure. Preheat the grill, with the lid closed, to 250°F.

2.   Generously season the pork belly cubes with the rub. Using your hands, work the rub into the meat

3.   Place the pork cubes directly on the grill grate and smoke until their internal temperature reaches 195°F.

4.	Transfer the cubes from the grill to an aluminum pan. Add the honey, barbecue sauce, and brown sugar. Stir to combine and coat the pork.

5.	Place the pan in the grill and smoke the pork for 1 hour, uncovered. Remove the pork from the grill and serve immediately.

Nutrition: Calories: 1301 Fat: 124g Saturated Fat: 46g

Chicken Fajitas on a Traeger Grill

Preparation Time: 10 minutes

Cooking Time: 40 minutes Servings: 1

Ingredients:

- 2 lbs. Chicken breast, thin sliced
- 1 large Red bell pepper
- 1 large Onion
- 1 large Orange bell pepper
- Seasoning mix
- 2 tbsp. Oil
- ½ tbsp. Onion powder
- ½ tbsp. Granulated garlic
- 1 tbsp. Salt

Directions:

1. Preheat the grill to 450°F.
2. Mix the seasonings and oil.
3. Add the chicken slices to the mix.
4. Line a large pan with a non-stick baking sheet.
5. Let the pan heat for 10 minutes.

6.   Place the chicken, peppers, and other vegetables on the grill. Grill for 10 minutes or until the chicken is cooked.

7.   Remove it from the grill and serve with warm tortillas and vegetables.

Nutrition: Carbs: 5 g   Protein: 29 g Fat: 6 g   Sodium: 360 mg Cholesterol: 77 mg

Smoked Turkey Patties

Preparation Time: 20 minutes

Cooking Time: 40 minutes

Servings: 6

Ingredients:

- 2 lbs. turkey minced meat

- ½ cup parsley finely chopped

- 2⁄3 cup onion finely chopped

- 1 red bell pepper finely chopped

- 1 large egg at room temperature

- Salt and pepper to taste

- ½ tsp. dry oregano

- ½ tsp. dry thyme

Directions:

1. In a bowl, combine well all ingredients.

2. Make from the mixture patties.

3. Start traeger grill on (recommended apple or oak traeger) lid open, until the fire is established (4–5 minutes). Increase the temperature to 350°F and allow to pre-heat, lid closed, for 10–15 minutes.

4.   Place patties on the grill racks and cook with lid covered for 30 to 40 minutes.

5.   Your turkey patties are ready when you reach a temperature of 130°FServe hot.

Nutrition: Calories: 251 arbs: 3.4g Fat: 12.5 Fiber: 0.9g Protein: 31.2g

Smoked Pork Sausages

Preparation Time: 10 minutes

Cooking Time: 1 hour

Servings: 6

Ingredients:

- 3 pounds ground pork
- ½ tbsp. ground mustard
- 1 tbsp. onion powder
- 1 tbsp. garlic powder
- 1 tsp. pink curing salt
- 1 tsp. salt
- 1 tsp. black pepper
- ¼ cup ice water
- Hog casings, soaked and rinsed in cold water

Directions:

1. Mix all ingredients except for the hog casings in a bowl. Using your hands, mix until all ingredients are well-combined.

2. Using a sausage stuffer, stuff the hog casings with the pork mixture.

3.   Measure 4 inches of the stuffed hog casing and twist to form into a sausage. Repeat the process until you create sausage links.

4.   When ready to cook, fire the Traeger Grill to 225°F. Use apple traeger when cooking the ribs. Close the lid and preheat for 15 minutes.

5.   Place the sausage links on the grill grate and cook for 1 hour or until the internal temperature reads at 155°F.

6.   Allow resting before slicing.

Nutrition:

• Calories: 688

• Protein: 58.9g

• Carbs: 2.7g

• Fat: 47.3g

• Sugar: 0.2g

Apple Smoked Turkey

Preparation Time: 30 Minutes

Cooking Time: 3 Hours

Servings: 5

Ingredients:

- 4 Cups Applewood chips
- 1 Fresh or frozen turkey about 12 pounds
- 3 Tbsp. extra-virgin olive oil
- 1 tbsp. chopped fresh sage
- 2 and ½ tsp. kosher salt
- 2 tsp. freshly ground black pepper
- 1 and ½ tsp. paprika
- 1 tsp. chopped fresh thyme
- 1 tsp. chopped fresh oregano
- 1 tsp. garlic powder
- 1 cup water
- ½ cup chopped onion
- ½ cup chopped carrot
- ½ cup chopped celery

Directions:

1.   Soak the wood chips into the water for about 1 hour; then drain very well.

2.   Remove the neck and the giblets from the turkey; then reserve and discard the liver. Pat the turkey dry; then trim any excess of fat and start at the neck's cavity

3.   Loosen the skin from the breast and the drumstick by inserting your fingers and gently push it between the meat and skin and lift the wingtips, then over back and tuck under the turkey

4.   Combine the oil and the next 7 ingredients in a medium bowl and rub the oil under the skin; then rub it over the breasts and the drumsticks

5.   Tie the legs with the kitchen string.

6.   Pour 1 cup of water, the onion, the carrot, and the celery into the bottom of an aluminum foil roasting pan

7.   Place the roasting rack into a pan; then arrange the turkey with the breast side up over a roasting rack; then let stand at room temperature for about 1 hour

8.   Remove the grill rack; then preheat the charcoal smoker grill to medium-high heat.

9. After preheating the smoker to a temperature of about 225°F Place 2 cups of wood chips on the heating element on the right side.

10. Replace the grill rack; then place the roasting pan with the turkey over the grill rack over the left burner.

11. Cover and smoke for about 3 hours and turn the chicken halfway through the cooking time; then add the remaining 2 cups of wood chips halfway through the cooking time.

12. Place the turkey over a cutting board; then let stand for about 30 minutes

13. Discard the turkey skin; then serve and enjoy your dish!

Nutrition: Calories: 530 Fat: 22g Carbs: 14g Protein: 41g Fiber: 2g

Cajun Doubled-Smoked Ham

Preparation Time: 20 minutes

Cooking Time: 4 to 5 hours

Servings: 10 to 12

Ingredients:

- 1 (5 or 6-pound) bone-in smoked ham

- 1 batch Cajun Rub

- 3 tbsp. honey

Directions:

1. Supply your smoker with a traeger and follow the manufacturer's specific start-up procedure. Preheat the grill, with the lid closed, to 225°F.

2. Generously season the ham with the rub and place it either in a pan or directly on the grill grate. Smoke it for 1 hour.

3. Drizzle the honey over the ham and continue to smoke it until the ham's internal temperature reaches 145°F.

4. Remove the ham from the grill and let it rest for 5 to 10 minutes before thinly slicing and serving.

Nutrition:

- Calories: 60

- Saturated Fat: 0.5g

- Cholesterol: 25mg

- Carbs 2g

Bacon Grilled Cheese Sandwich

Preparation Time: 15 minutes Cooking Time: 5 minutes

Servings: 4 Ingredients:

- 1 lb. Applewood Smoked Bacon Slices, Cooked

- 8 Slices Texas Toast

- 16 Slices Cheddar Cheese

- Mayonnaise

- Butter

Directions:

1. When ready to cook, set the temperature to 350°F and preheat, lid closed for 15 minutes.

2. Spread a little bit of mayonnaise on each piece of bread, place 1 piece of cheddar on a slice then top with a couple of slices of bacon. Add another slice of cheese, then top with the other piece of bread. Spread softened butter on the exterior of the top piece of bread.

3. When the grill is hot, place the grilled cheese directly on a cleaned, oiled grill grate buttered side down. Then spread softened butter on the exterior of the top slice.

4.   Cook the grilled cheese on the first side for 5–7 minutes until grill marks develop and the cheese has begun to melt. Flip the sandwich and repeat on the other side.

5.   Remove from the grill when the cheese is melted, and the exterior is lightly toasted. Enjoy!

Nutrition: Calories: 500 Carbs: 30g Fat: 29g Protein: 28g

Recipe Spare Ribs

Preparation Time: 15 minutes

Cooking Time: 2 hours

Servings: 4

Ingredients:

- spareribs

- 1500 grams spareribs

- 2 tbsp. mustard

- 3 tbsp. Mother all rubs

- 4 tbsp. Cola BBQ Sauce

- 25 grams butter

Supplies:

- 4 aluminum containers

- BBQ with lid

- 2 chunks smoking wood apple

- Aluminum foil

Directions:

1. Rinse the ribs well, pat them dry and remove the fleece.

Make sure you use a handy knife for this (no sharp point).

Make an opening by sliding the knife between the fleeces and carefully unravel the fleece.

2.   Use your fingers for this, but you can also use the knife. Make sure you don't damage the meat itself by running your knife only along the bone (and not along with the meat).

3.   Cut off loose pieces of meat and fat at the top and cut the ribs in half.

4.   Coat the bottom with mustard and sprinkle with half of the rub. Flip the ribs and grease the top with mustard as well and sprinkle with the other half of the rub.

5.   Prepare the BBQ for indirect grilling at a temperature of 110°. Add the smoking wood to the coals as soon as the BBQ is up to temperature.

6.   Place the ribs on the BBQ (the indirect part) and smoke the ribs for about an hour.

7.   Place the ribs all in a separate aluminum container, add a small knob of butter and wrap the containers tightly with aluminum foil so that no more air can reach.

8.   Place the ribs in the trays on the BBQ for another two hours.

9. Remove the ribs from the containers and place them on the wire rack on the indirect part for another 20 minutes and brush the ribs with barbecue sauce.

10. Ready and enjoy!

Tip:

For anyone who prefers not to eat pork, you can also replace the spare ribs with veal spare ribs. These are slightly less fat but also have a very tasty taste.

Nutrition:

- Calories: 167 Fat: 20g

- Carbs: 24g Fiber: 1.3 g

- Protein: 12.1g

Thanksgiving Dinner Turkey

Preparation Time: 15 minutes

Cooking Time: 4 hours Servings: 16

Ingredients:

- ½ lb. butter, softened

- 2 tbsp. fresh thyme, chopped

- 2 tbsp. fresh rosemary, chopped

- 6 garlic cloves, crushed

- 1 (20-lb.) whole turkey, neck and giblets removed

- Salt and ground black pepper

Directions:

1. Set the temperature of the Grill to 300°F and preheat with a closed lid for 15 mins, using charcoal.

2. In a bowl, place butter, fresh herbs, garlic, salt, and black pepper and mix well.

3. Separate the turkey skin from the breast to create a pocket.

4. Stuff the breast pocket with a ¼-inch thick layer of butter mixture.

5. Season turkey with salt and black pepper.

6.   Arrange the turkey onto the grill and cook for 3-4 hours.

7.   Remove the turkey from the grill and place onto a cutting board for about 15-20 mins before carving.

8.   Cut the turkey into desired-sized pieces and serve.

Nutrition: Calories: 965 Carbs: 0.6 Protein: 106.5g Fat: 52g Sugar: 0g Sodium: 1916mg Fiber: 0.2g

Traeger Sheet Pan Chicken Fajitas

Preparation Time: 10 minutes Cooking Time: 10 minutes

Servings: 10

Ingredients:

- 2 lb. chicken breast

- 1 onion, sliced

- 1 red bell pepper, seeded and sliced

- 1 orange-red bell pepper, seeded and sliced

- 1 tbsp. salt

- ½ tbsp. onion powder

- ½ tbsp. granulated garlic

- 2 tbsp. Spiceologist Chile Margarita Seasoning

- 2 tbsp. oil

Directions:

1.   Preheat the Traeger to 450°F and line a baking sheet with parchment paper. In a mixing bowl, combine seasonings and oil then toss with the peppers and chicken.

2.   Place the baking sheet in the Traeger and let heat for 10 minutes with the lid closed.

3.   Open the lid and place the veggies and the chicken in a single layer. Close the lid and cook for 10 minutes or until the chicken is no longer pink.

4.   Serve with warm tortillas and top with your favorite toppings.

Nutrition:Calories: 211, Fat: 6g, Protein: 29g, Fiber: 1g, Sodium: 360mg

Buttered Thanksgiving Turkey

Preparation Time: 25 minutes Cooking Time: 5 or 6 hours

Servings: 12 to 14   Ingredients:

- 1 whole turkey (make sure the turkey is not pre-brined)

- 2 batches Garlic Butter Injectable

- 3 tbsp. olive oil

- 1 batch Chicken Rub

- 2 tbsp. butter

Directions:

1.   Supply your smoker with traegers and follow the manufacturer's specific start-up procedure. Preheat the grill, with the lid closed, to 180°F.

2.   Inject the turkey throughout with the garlic butter injectable. Coat the turkey with olive oil and season it with the rub. Using your hands, work the rub into the meat and skin.

3.   Place the turkey directly on the grill grate and smoke for 3 or 4 hours (for an 8- to 12-pound turkey, cook for 3 hours; for a turkey over 12 pounds, cook for 4 hours), basting it with butter every hour.

4.   Increase the grill's temperature to 375°F and continue to cook until the turkey's internal temperature reaches 170°F.

5.   Remove the turkey from the grill and let it rest for 10 minutes, before carving and serving.

Nutrition: Calories: 97cal Fat: 4 g Protein: 13 g Carbs: 1 g Fiber: 0 g

Apple Cider Braised Smoked BBQ Pulled Pork

Preparation Time: 20 minutes

Cooking Time: 6 to 7 hours

Servings: 4

Ingredients:

- 7–9 lb. bone-in pork butt/shoulder roast

RUB

- 4 tbsp. brown sugar

- 1 tbsp. garlic powder

- 1 tbsp. onion powder

- 1 tbsp. kosher salt

- ½ tbsp. pepper

- 1.5 tbsp. smoked paprika

- 2 tsp. dry mustard

- 1 tbsp. coriander

- 1 tbsp. chili powder

SPRAY

- ½ cup apple cider

- ½ cup apple cider vinegar

BRAISING

- 2 cups apple cider
- 3–4 sweet, crisp red apples, peeled and sliced
- 2 onions, sliced

SAUCE

- 1 cup ketchup
- ½ cup apple jelly
- ¼ cup apple cider
- 1 tbsp. apple cider vinegar
- 1 tsp. liquid smoke
- ½ tbsp. Worcestershire sauce
- 1 tsp. chili powder
- ½ tsp. onion powder
- 1 cup pan juices from the roast (fat separated)

Directions:

1. Pat roast dry. Combine all rub ingredients and a pat on all sides of the roast, rubbing in well. Cover roast and let sit overnight in the fridge.

2. When ready to cook, preheat smoker to 225°F and smoke roast directly on the grill for 5 hours. While cooking,

combine spray ingredients in a clean spray bottle and spritz roast all over once every hour.

3.   While roast is smoking, combine all sauce ingredients and whisk them together in a pan. Set aside until pan juices are ready.

4.   After smoking, transfer your roast to either your slow cooker (if it fits, remember you have more stuff going in there!) or a roasting pan or disposable roasting pan (if you'll continue cooking on the smoker.)

5.   Place apples, onions, and 2 cups of apple cider around the roast in the roasting pan. Cover with a lid or tightly with foil. Cook in the slow cooker on high for 6–7 hours (or low for more like 8–10 if you want/need to drag it out, overnight, for example.) If you are cooking in the oven, set the temperature to 275°F. In the smoker, you can increase the temperature to 275°F as well. Cook until internal temperature reaches 200–210 degrees, usually about 6–7 hours.

6.   Let pork rest, covered for at least 15 minutes (longer is just fine) before discarding bones, separating fat, etc.

7.   Pour pan juices into a fat separator. Pour 1 cup of juices into your BBQ sauce and bring to a simmer. Simmer for about 15 minutes until slightly thickened.

8.   Pour a little of the remaining juices over shredded pork. Use a slotted spoon to grab the onions and apples and mix them in with the pork. Serve alone or on rolls or over rice. Freezes great! Excellent on nachos, pizzas, and more.

Nutrition:

- Calories: 426;

- Protein: 65.3g;

- Carbs: 20.4g;

- Fat: 8.4g

- sugar: 17.8g

Honey Baked Mustard Chicken

Preparation Time: 15 minutes

Cooking Time: 35 minutes

Servings: 4

Ingredients:

- 4 boneless skinless chicken breasts (4 ounces each)

- 1 tbsp. grainy mustard

- 4 tbsp. honey

- ½ tsp. white vinegar

- ½ tsp. paprika

- 2 tbsp. Dijon mustard

- 1 tbsp. + 2 tsp. olive oil

- 1 tsp. salt

- 1 tsp. ground black pepper or to taste

- 1 tbsp. freshly chopped parsley

- 1 tsp. dried basil

Directions:

1.   Preheat the traeger grill to 375°F with the lid closed for 15 minutes.

2.   Grease a baking dish with a non-stick cooking spray.

3.   Season both sides of the chicken breasts with pepper and salt.

4.   Place a cast-iron skillet on the grill and add 2 tsp. olive oil.

5.   Once the oil is hot, add the seasoned chicken breast, sauté until both sides of the chicken breasts are browned.

6.   Use a slotted spoon to transfer the fried chicken breast to a paper towel lined plate.

7.   Combine the Dijon mustard, honey, vinegar, basil, grainy mustard, remaining oil, paprika in a mixing bowl. Mix until the ingredients are well combined.

8.   Pour half of the honey mixture into the prepared baking dish, spread it to cover the bottom of the dish.

9.   Arrange the chicken breast into the dish and pour the remaining honey mixture over the chicken.

10.   Cover the baking dish with foil and place it on the grill. Cook on grill for about 20 minutes.

11.   Remove the foil cover and cook, uncovered, for 15 minutes.

12. Remove the baking dish from the grill and let the chicken cool for a few minutes.

Nutrition:

- Calories: 320

- Fat 12.4g

- Carbs: 18.5g

- Fiber: 0.6g

- Protein: 33.4g

Bourbon Honey Glazed Smoked Pork Ribs

Preparation Time: 15 minutes

Cooking Time: 5 hours Servings: 10

Ingredients:

- Pork Ribs (4-lbs., 1.8-kg.)

The Marinade

- 1 ½ cups Apple juice

- ½ cup Yellow mustard

The Rub

- ¼ cup Brown Sugar

- 1 tbsp. Smoked paprika

- ¾ tbsp. Onion powder

- ¾ tbsp. Garlic powder

- 1 tsp. Chili powder

- ¾ tsp. Cayenne pepper

- 1 ½ tsp. Salt

The Glaze

- 2 tbsp. Unsalted butter

- ¼ cup Honey

- 3 tbsp. Bourbon

Directions:

1. Place apple juice and yellow mustard in a bowl, then stir until combined.

2. Apply the mixture over the pork ribs, then marinates for at least an hour.

3. In the meantime, combine brown Sugar: with smoked paprika, onion powder, garlic powder, chili powder, black pepper, cayenne pepper, and salt, then mix well.

4. After an hour of the marinade, sprinkle the dry spice mixture over the marinated pork ribs, then let it rest for a few minutes.

5. Plug the traeger grill smoker, then fill the hopper with the wood pellet. Turn the switch on.

6. Set the traeger smoker for indirect heat, then adjust the temperature to 250°F (121°C).

7. When the traeger smoker is ready, place the seasoned pork ribs in the traeger smoker and smoke for 3 hours.

8. Meanwhile, place unsalted butter in a saucepan, then melt over very low heat. Once it is melted, remove it from

heat, and then add honey and bourbon to the saucepan. Stir until incorporated and set aside. After 3 hours of smoking, baste the honey bourbon mixture over the pork ribs and wrap it with aluminum foil.

9.   Return the wrapped pork ribs to the traeger smoker and continue smoking for another 2 hours.

10.   Once the smoked pork ribs reach 145°F (63°C), remove the smoked pork ribs from the traeger grill smoker.

11.   Unwrap the smoked pork ribs and serve.

Nutrition: Calories: 313 Carbs: 5g Fat: 20g Protein: 26g

Bacon Wrapped Turkey Legs

Preparation Time: 10 minutes

Cooking Time: 3 hours

Servings: 4-6

Ingredients:

- Gallon water

- traeger rub, to taste

- ½ cup pink curing salt

- ½ cup brown Sugar:

- 6 whole peppercorns

- 2 whole dried bay leaves

- ½ gallon ice water

- 8 whole turkey legs

- 16 sliced bacon

Directions:

1.   In a large stockpot, mix one gallon of water, the rub, curing salt, brown sugar, peppercorns, and bay leaves.

2.   Boil it over high heat to dissolve the salt and Sugar: granules. Take off the heat then add in ½ gallon of ice and water.

3. The brine must be at least to room temperature, if not colder.

4. Place the turkey legs, completely submerged in the brine.

5. After 24 hours, drain the turkey legs then remove the brine.

6. Wash the brine off the legs with cold water, then dry thoroughly with paper towels.

7. When ready to cook, start the traeger grill according to grill instructions. Set the heat to 250°F and preheat, lid closed for 10 to 15 minutes.

8. Place turkey legs directly on the grill grate.

9. After 2 ½ hours, wrap a piece of bacon around each leg then finish cooking them for 30 to 40 minutes of smoking.

10. The total smoking time for the legs will be 3 hours or until the internal temperature reaches 165°F on an instant-read meat thermometer. Serve, Enjoy!

Nutrition:

- Calories: 390

- Fat: 14g

- Saturated Fat: 0g

- Cholesterol: 64mg

- Sodium: 738mg

- Carbs: 44g

BBQ Spareribs with Mandarin Glaze

Preparation Time: 10 minutes

Cooking Time: 60 minutes

Servings: 6

Ingredients:

- 3 large spareribs, membrane removed

- 3 tbsp. yellow mustard

- 1 tbsp. Worcestershire sauce

- 1 cup honey

- 1 ½ cup brown Sugar:

- 13 ounces Traeger Mandarin Glaze

- 1 tsp. sesame oil

- 1 tsp. soy sauce

- 1 tsp. garlic powder

Directions:

1.   Place the spareribs on a working surface and carefully remove the connective tissue membrane that covers the ribs.

2.   In another bowl, mix the rest of the ingredients until well combined.

3.　　Massage the spice mixture onto the spareribs. Allow resting in the fridge for at least 3 hours.

4.　　When ready to cook, fire the Traeger Grill to 300°F.

5.　　Use hickory traeger when cooking the ribs.

6.　　Close the lid and preheat for 15 minutes.

7.　　Place the seasoned ribs on the grill grate and cover the lid.

8.　　Cook for 60 minutes.

9.　　Once cooked, allow resting before slicing.

Nutrition:

- Calories: 1263

- Protein: 36.9g

- Carbs: 110.3g

- Fat: 76.8g

- Sugar: 107g

Juicy Beer Can Turkey

Preparation Time: 20 Minutes

Cooking Time: 6 hours

Servings: 6-8

Ingredients:

For the rub

- 4 garlic cloves, minced

- 2 tsp. dry ground mustard

- 2 tsp. smoked paprika

- 2 tsp. salt

- 2 tsp. freshly ground black pepper

- 1 tsp. ground cumin

- 1 tsp. ground turmeric

- 1 tsp. onion powder

- ½ tsp. Sugar

For the turkey

- (10-pound) fresh whole turkey, neck, giblets, and gizzard removed and discarded

- tbsp. olive oil

- 1 large, wide (24-ounce) can of beer, such as Foster's

- 4 dried bay leaves

- 2 tsp. ground sage

- 2 tsp. dried thyme

- ¼ cup (½ stick) unsalted butter, melted

Directions:

To make the rub

1. Following the manufacturer's specific start-up procedure, preheat the smoker to 250°F, and add cherry, peach, or apricot wood.

2. In a small bowl, stir together the garlic, mustard, paprika, salt, pepper, cumin, turmeric, onion powder, and sugar.

To make the turkey

1. Rub the turkey inside and out with olive oil.

2. Apply the spice rub all over the turkey.

3. Pour out or drink 12 ounces of the beer.

4. Using a can opener, remove the entire top of the beer can.

5. Add the bay leaves, sage, and thyme to the beer.

6.   Place the can of beer upright on the smoker grate. Carefully fit the turkey over it until the entire can is inside the cavity and the bird stands by itself. Prop the legs forward to aid in stability.

7.   Smoke the turkey for 6 hours, basting with the butter every other hour.

8.   Remove the turkey from the heat when the skin is browned and the internal temperature registers 165°F. Remove the beer can very carefully—it will be slippery, and the liquid inside extremely hot. Discard the liquid, and recycle the can.

9.   Let the turkey rest for 20 minutes before carving.

Nutrition: Calories: 300 Fat: 12g Carbs: 1g Fiber: 0g Protein: 42g

Vegetables and Vegetarian Recipes

Georgia Sweet Onion Bake

Preparation Time: 10 Minutes Cooking Time: 30 Minutes

Servings: 4 Ingredients:

- 4 large Vidalia or other sweet onions

- 8 tbsp. (1 stick) unsalted butter, melted

- 4 chicken bouillon cubes

- 1 cup grated Parmesan cheese

Directions:

1. Supply your smoker with Traeger and follow the manufacturer's specific start-up procedure. Preheat, with the lid closed, to 350°F.

2. Coat a high-sided baking pan with cooking spray or butter.

3. Peel the onions and cut them into quarters, separating them into individual petals.

4. Spread the onions out in the prepared pan and pour the melted butter over them.

5. Crush the bouillon cubes and sprinkle over the buttery onion pieces, and then top with the cheese.

6.   Transfer the pan to the grill, close the lid, and smoke for 30 minutes. Remove the pan from the grill, cover tightly with aluminum foil, and poke several holes all over to vent.

7.   Place the pan back on the grill, close the lid, and smoke for an additional 30 to 45 minutes.

8.   Uncover the onions, stir, and serve hot.

Nutrition: Calories: 50 Carbs: 4g Fiber: 2g Fat: 2.5g Protein: 2g

Traeger Grilled Vegetables

Preparation Time: 5 minutes

Cooking Time: 15 minutes

Servings: 8

Ingredients:

- 1 veggie tray

- ¼ cup vegetable oil

- 2 tbsp. veggie seasoning

Directions:

1. Preheat the Traeger grill to 375°F

2. Toss the vegetables in oil then place on a sheet pan.

3. Sprinkle with veggie seasoning then place on the hot grill.

4. Grill for 15 minutes or until the veggies are cooked

5. Let rest then serve. Enjoy.

Nutrition:

- Calories: 44

- Fat: 5g

- Saturated Fat: 0g

- Carbs: 1g

- Net Carbs: 1g

- Sodium: 36mg

- Potassium: 10mg

Roasted Okra

Preparation Time: 10 Minutes Cooking Time: 30 Minutes

Servings: 4 Ingredients:

- 1-pound whole okra

- 2 tbsp. extra-virgin olive oil

- 2 tsp. seasoned salt

- 2 tsp. freshly ground black pepper

Directions:

1. Supply your smoker with Traeger and follow the manufacturer's specific start-up procedure. Preheat, with the lid closed, to 400°F. Alternatively, preheat your oven to 400°F.

2. Line a shallow rimmed baking pan with aluminum foil and coat with cooking spray.

3. Arrange the okra on the pan in a single layer. Drizzle with the olive oil, turning to coat. Season on all sides with salt and pepper.

4. Place the baking pan on the grill grate, close the lid, and smoke for 30 minutes, or until crisp and slightly charred. Alternatively, roast in the oven for 30 minutes.

5.   Serve hot.

Smoking Tip: Whether you make this okra in the oven or in your Traeger grill, be sure to fully preheat the oven or cook chamber for the best results.

Nutrition: Calories: 150 Carbs: 15 g Protein: 79 g Sodium: 45 mg Cholesterol: 49 mg

Traeger Grilled Asparagus and Honey Glazed Carrots

Preparation Time: 15 minutes

Cooking Time: 35 minutes

Servings: 5

Ingredients:

- 1 bunch asparagus, trimmed ends

- 1 lb. carrots, peeled

- 2 tbsp. olive oil

- Sea salt to taste

- 2 tbsp. honey

- Lemon zest

Directions:

1. Sprinkle the asparagus with oil and sea salt. Drizzle the carrots with honey and salt.

2. Preheat the Traeger to 165°F with the lid closed for 15 minutes.

3. Place the carrots in the Traeger and cook for 15 minutes. Add asparagus and cook for 20 more minutes or until cooked through.

4.   Top the carrots and asparagus with lemon zest. Enjoy.

Nutrition:

- Calories: 1680 Fat: 30g Saturated Fat: 2g

- Carbs: 10g Net Carbs: 10g

- Protein: 4g Sodium: 514mg

Fish & Seafood Recipes

Grilled Calamari with Mustard Oregano and Parsley Sauce

Preparation Time: 10 minutes

Cooking Time: 35 minutes

Servings: 6

Ingredients:

- 8 Calamari, cleaned

- 2 cups milk

- Sauce

- 4 tsp. sweet mustard

- Juice from 2 lemons

- ½ cup olive oil

- 2 tbsp. fresh oregano, finely chopped

- Pepper, ground

- ½ bunch parsley, finely chopped

Intolerances:

- Gluten-Free

- Egg-Free

- Lactose-Free

Directions:

1.   Clean calamari well and cut into slices.

2.   Place calamari in a large metal bow, cover, and marinate with milk overnight.

3.   Remove calamari from the milk and drain well on a paper towel. Grease the fish lightly with olive oil.

4.   In a bowl, combine mustard and the juice from the two lemons.

5.   Beat lightly and pour the olive oil very slowly; stir until all the ingredients are combined well.

6.   Add the oregano and pepper and stir well.

7.   Start the Traeger grill and set the temperature to moderate; preheat, lid closed, for 10 to 15 minutes.

8.   Place the calamari on the grill and cook for 2-3 minutes per side or until it has a bit of char and remove from the grill.

9.   Transfer calamari to serving platter and pour them over with mustard sauce and chopped parsley.

Nutrition:

- Calories: 212

- Fat: 19g

- Cholesterol: 651mg

- Carbs: 7g

- Protein: 3g

Grilled Trout in White Wine and Parsley Marinade

Preparation Time: 20 minutes

Cooking Time: 45 minutes

Servings: 4

Ingredients:

- ¼ cup olive oil

- 1 lemon juice

- ½ cup white wine

- 2 cloves garlic minced

- 2 tbsp. fresh parsley, finely chopped

- 1 tsp. fresh basil, finely chopped

- Salt and freshly ground black pepper to taste

- 4 trout fish, cleaned

- Lemon slices for garnish

Intolerances:

- Gluten-Free

- Egg-Free

- Lactose-Free

Directions:

1.   In a large container, stir olive oil, lemon juice, wine, garlic, parsley, basil and salt, and freshly ground black pepper to taste.

2.   Submerge fish in sauce and toss to combine well.

3.   Cover and marinate in refrigerate overnight.

4.   When ready to cook, start the Traeger grill on Smoke with the lid open for 4 to 5 minutes. Set the temperature to 400°F and preheat, lid closed, for 10 to 15 minutes.

5.   Remove the fish from marinade and pat dry on a paper towel; reserve marinade.

6.   Grill trout for 5 minutes from both sides (be careful not to overcook the fish).

7.   Pour fish with marinade and serve hot with lemon slices.

Nutrition:

- Calories: 267

- Fat: 18g

- Carbs: 3g

- Protein: 16g

Grilled Cuttlefish with Spinach and Pine Nuts Salad

Preparation Time: 15 minutes

Cooking Time: 30 minutes

Servings: 6

Ingredients:

- ½ cup olive oil

- 1 tbsp. lemon juice

- 1 tsp. oregano

- Pinch salt

- 8 large cuttlefish, cleaned

- Spinach, pine nuts, olive oil, and vinegar for serving

Intolerances:

- Gluten-Free

- Egg-Free

- Lactose-Free

Directions:

1. Prepare the marinade with olive oil, lemon juice, oregano, and a pinch of salt pepper (be careful, cuttlefish do not need too much salt).

2.   Place the cuttlefish in the marinade, tossing to cover evenly. Cover and marinate for about 1 hour.

3.   Remove the cuttlefish from the marinade and pat dry them on a paper towel.

4.   Start the Traeger grill, and set the temperature to high, and preheat, lid closed, for 10 to 15 minutes.

5.   Grill the cuttlefish for just 3 - 4 minutes on each side.

6.   Serve hot with spinach, pine nuts, olive oil, and vinegar.

Nutrition:

- Calories: 299

- Fat: 19g

- Cholesterol: 186mg

- Carbs: 3g

- Protein: 28g

Grilled Dijon Lemon Catfish Fillets

Preparation Time: 15 minutes

Cooking Time: 25 minutes

Servings: 6

Ingredients:

- ½ cup olive oil

- Juice 4 lemons

- 2 tbsp. Dijon mustard

- ½ tsp. salt

- 1 tsp. paprika

- Fresh rosemary chopped

- 4 (6- to 8-oz.) catfish fillets, ½-inch thick

Intolerances:

- Gluten-Free

- Egg-Free

- Lactose-Free

Directions:

1.   Set the temperature to Medium and preheat, lid closed, for 10 to 15 minutes.

2.   Whisk the olive oil, lemon juice, mustard, salt, paprika, and chopped rosemary in a bowl.

3.   Brush one side of each fish fillet with half of the olive oil-lemon mixture; season with salt and pepper to taste.

4.   Grill fillets, covered, 4 to 5 minutes. Turn fillets and brush with the remaining olive oil-lemon mixture.

5.   Grill 4 to 5 minutes more (do not cover).

6.   Remove fish fillets to a serving platter, sprinkle with rosemary and serve.

Nutrition:

- Calories: 295

- Fat: 24g

- Cholesterol: 58mg

- Carbs: 3g

- Protein: 16g

Grilled Halibut Fillets in Chili Rosemary Marinade

Preparation Time: 15 minutes

Cooking Time: 55 minutes

Servings: 6

Ingredients:

- 1 cup virgin olive oil

- 2 large red chili peppers, chopped

- 2 cloves garlic, cut into quarters

- 1 bay leaf

- 1 twig rosemary

- 2 lemons

- 4 tbsp. white vinegar

- 4 halibut fillets

Intolerances:

- Gluten-Free

- Egg-Free

- Lactose-Free

Directions:

1.   In a large container, mix olive oil, chopped red chili, garlic, bay leaf, rosemary, lemon juice, and white vinegar.

2.   Submerge halibut fillets and toss to combine well.

3.   Cover and marinate in the refrigerator for several hours or overnight.

4.   Remove anchovies from marinade and pat dry on paper towels for 30 minutes.

5.   Start the Traeger grill, set the temperature to medium, and preheat, lid closed for 10 to 15 minutes.

6.   Grill the anchovies, skin side down for about 10 minutes, or until the flesh of the fish becomes white (thinner cuts and fillets can cook in as little time as 6 minutes).

7.   Turn once during cooking to avoid having the halibut fall apart.

8.   Transfer to a large serving platter, pour a little lemon juice over the fish, sprinkle with rosemary and serve.

Nutrition:

- Calories: 259

- Fat: 4g

- Cholesterol: 133mg

- Carbs: 5g

- Protein: 51g

Grilled Lobster with Lemon Butter and Parsley

Preparation Time: 15 minutes

Cooking Time: 40 minutes

Servings: 4

Ingredients:

- 1 lobster (or more)

- ½ cup fresh butter

- 2 lemons juice (freshly squeezed)

- 2 tbsp. parsley

- Salt and freshly ground pepper to taste

Intolerances:

- Gluten-Free

- Egg-Free

Directions:

1. Use a pot large enough large to hold the lobsters and fill water and salt. Bring to boil and put in lobster. Boil for 4 - 5 minutes.

2. Remove lobster to the working surface.

3.   Pull the body to the base of the head and divide the head.

4.   Firmly hold the body, with the abdomen upward, and with a sharp knife cut it along in the middle.

5.   Start your Traeger grill with the lid open until the fire is established (4 to 5 minutes). Set the temperature to 350°F and preheat, lid closed for 10 to 15 minutes.

6.   Melt the butter and beat it with lemon juice, parsley, salt, and pepper. Spread butter mixture over lobster and put directly on a grill grate.

7.   Grill lobsters cut side down about 7 - 8 minutes until the shells are bright in color (also, depends on their size).

8.   Turn the lobster over and brush with butter mixture. Grill for another 4 - 5 minutes.

9.   Serve hot sprinkled with lemon butter and parsley finely chopped.

Nutrition:

• Calories: 385

• Fat: 24g

• Cholesterol: 346mg

- Carbs: 2g

- Protein: 37g

Rub and Sauces Recipes

Smoked Sriracha Sauce

Preparation Time: 10 minutes Cooking Time: 1 hour

Servings: 2 Ingredients:

- 1 lb. Fresno chilies stem pulled off and seeds removed

- ½ cup rice vinegar

- ½ cup red wine vinegar

- 1 carrot, medium and cut into rounds, ¼ inch

- 1-½ tbsp. sugar, dark brown

- 4 garlic cloves, peeled

- 1 tbsp. olive oil

- 1 tbsp. kosher salt

- ½ cup water

Directions:

1. Smoke chilies in a smoker for about 15 minutes.

2. Bring to boil both kinds of vinegar then add carrots, sugar, and garlic. Simmer for about 15 minutes while covered. Cool for 30 minutes.

3. Place the chilies, olive oil, vinegar-vegetable mixture, salt, and ¼ cup water into a blender.

4.   Blend for about 1-2 minutes on high. Add remaining water and blend again. You can add another ¼ cup water if you want your sauce thinner. Pour the sauce into jars and place in a refrigerator. Serve.

Nutrition: Calories: 147   Fat: 5.23g Carbs: 21g rotein: 3g Fiber: 3g

Cheese and Breads

Low Carb Almond Flour Bread

Preparation Time: 10 minutes

Cooking Time: 1 hour 15 minutes

Servings: 24 slices

Ingredients:

- 1tsp. sea salt or to taste

- 1tbsp. apple cider vinegar

- ½ cup warm water

- ¼ cup coconut oil

- 4large eggs (beaten)

- 1tbsp. gluten-free baking powder

- 2cup blanched almond flour

- ¼ cup Psyllium husk powder

- 1tsp. ginger (optional)

Directions:

1. Preheat the grill to 350°F with the lid closed for 15 minutes.

2.   Line a 9 by 5-inch loaf pan with parchment paper. Set aside.

3.   Combine the ginger, Psyllium husk powder, almond flour, salt, baking powder in a large mixing bowl.

4.   In another mixing bowl, mix the coconut oil, apple cider vinegar, eggs, and warm water. Mix thoroughly.

5.   Gradually pour the flour mixture into the egg mixture, stirring as you pour. Stir until it forms a smooth batter.

6.   Fill the lined loaf pan with the batter and cover the batter with aluminum foil.

7.   Place the loaf pan directly on the grill and bake for about 1 hour or until a toothpick or knife inserted in the middle of the bread comes out clean.

Nutrition:

- Calories: 93

- Fat: 7.5g

- Saturated Fat: 2.6g

- Cholesterol: 31mg

- Sodium: 139mg

- Carbs: 3.6g

- Fiber: 2.2g

- Sugars: 0.1g

- Protein: 3.1g

Traeger Grill Chicken Flatbread

Preparation Time: 5 minutes

Cooking Time: 30 minutes

Servings: 6

Ingredients:

- 6 mini breads

- 1-½ cups divided buffalo sauce

- 4 cups cooked and cubed chicken breasts

- For drizzling: mozzarella cheese

Directions:

1. Preheat your Traeger grill to 375 - 400°F.

2. Place the breads on a surface, flat, and then evenly spread ½ cup buffalo sauce on all breads.

3. Toss together chicken breasts and 1 cup buffalo sauce then top over all the pieces of bread evenly.

4. Top each with mozzarella cheese.

5. Place the pieces of bread directly on the grill but over indirect heat. Close the lid.

6. Cook for about 5-7 minutes until slightly toasty edges, cheese is melted and fully hated chicken. Remove and drizzle with ranch or blue cheese. Enjoy!

Nutrition:Calories: 346 Fat: 7.6g Saturated Fat: 2g Carbs: 33.9g Net Carbs: 32.3g Protein: 32.5g Sugars: 0.8g Fiber: 1.6g Sodium: 642mg

Nut, Fruits and Dessert

Apple Pie Grill

Preparation Time: 20 minutes

Cooking Time: 30 minutes

Servings: 4

Ingredients:

- ¼ cup sugar

- 4 apples, sliced

- 1tbsp. cornstarch

- 1tsp. cinnamon, ground

- 1pie crust, refrigerator, soften in according to the directions on the box

- ½ cup peach, preserves

Directions:

1. Preheat your smoker to 375°F, the closed lid

2. Take a bowl and add cinnamon, cornstarch, apples and keep it on the side

3. Place piecrust in pie pan and spread preserves, place apples

4. Fold crust slightly

5.   Place pan on your smoker (upside down), smoke for 30-40 minutes

6.   Once done, let it rest

7.   Serve and enjoy!

Nutrition: Calories: 160 Fats: 1g Carbs: 35g Fiber: 1g

Grilled Fruit with Cream

Preparation Time: 15 minutes

Cooking Time: 10min Servings: 4 - 6

Ingredients:

- 2 halved Apricot

- 1 halved Nectarine

- 1 halved peaches

- ¼ cup Blueberries

- ½ cup Raspberries

- 2 tbsp. Honey

- 1 orange, the peel

- 2 cups Cream

- ½ cup Balsamic Vinegar

Directions:

1.   Preheat the grill to 400°F with a closed lid.

2.   Grill the peaches, nectarines, and apricots for 4 minutes on each side. Place a pan over the stove and turn on medium heat. Add 2 tbsp. of honey, vinegar, and orange peel. Simmer until medium thick. Add honey and cream in a bowl. Whip until it reaches a soft form.

3.   Place the fruits on a serving plate. Sprinkle with berries. Drizzle with balsamic reduction.

4.   Serve with cream.

Nutrition: Calories: 230 Protein: 3g Fiber: 0g Carbs: 35g Fat: 3g

Lamb Recipes

Roasted Leg of Lamb

Preparation Time: 15 minutes

Cooking Time: 1-2 hours

Servings: 4

Ingredients:

- Traeger Flavor: Hickory

- 1 (6- to 8-pound) boneless leg of lamb

- 2 batches Rosemary-Garlic Lamb Seasoning

Directions:

1. Supply your smoker with Traeger and follow the manufacturer's specific start-up procedure. Preheat the grill to 350°F. Close the lid

2. Using your hands, rub the lamb leg with the seasoning, rubbing it under and around any netting.

3. Put the lamb directly on the grill grate and smoke until its internal temperature reaches 145°F.

4. Take off the lamb from the grill and let it rest for 20 to 30 minutes, before removing the netting, slicing, and serving.

Nutrition:

- Calories: 50

- Carbs: 4g

- Fiber: 2g

- Fat: 2.5g

- Protein: 2g

Smoked Lamb Sausage

Preparation Time: 2 hours

Cooking Time: 6 hours

Servings: 6

Ingredients:

Traegers:

- 1 tsp. cumin

- ½ tsp. cayenne pepper

- 1 tbsp. parsley

- 1 tsp. black pepper

- 1 Hog Casing

- 1 tbsp. garlic

- 1 tsp. paprika

- 2 tbsp. salt

- 2 tbsp. fennel, diced

- 1 tbsp. cilantro

- 2 lbs. lamb shoulders

- Cherry

Yogurt sauce:

- 3 cup yogurt

- Lemon juice to taste

- 1 clove garlic, minced

- Salt and pepper

- 1 cucumber, diced

- 1 onion, minced

Directions:

1. Chop the lamb into pieces before grinding the meat in a meat grinder.

2. Mix the lamb with all of the spices and refrigerate.

3. Then use a sausage horn to attach the hog casing and begin pushing the sausage through the grinder and into the casing, twisting into links. Make holes in the casing before refrigerating.

4. Mix all ingredients for the yogurt sauce and set aside.

5. When ready to cook, set your smoker to 225F and preheat.

6. Lay the sausage on the grill and smoke it for one hour.

7. Then, take the links off the grill and increase the grill's temperature to 500°F.

8.   Put the links back on the grill for 5 minutes on each side, and then serve with the yogurt sauce.

Nutrition:

- Calories: 50

- Carbs: 4g

- Fiber: 2g

- Fat: 2.5g

- Protein: 2g

Classic Lamb Chops

Preparation Time: 10 minutes

Cooking Time: 30 minutes

Servings: 4

Ingredients

- Traeger Flavor: Alder

- 4 (8-ounce) bone-in lamb chops

- 2 tbsp. olive oil

- 1 batch Rosemary-Garlic Lamb Seasoning

Directions:

1. Supply your smoker with Traeger and follow the manufacturer's specific start-up procedure. Preheat the grill to 350°F. Close the lid

2. Rub the lamb generously with olive oil and coat them on both sides with the seasoning.

3. Put the chops directly on the grill grate and grill until their internal temperature reaches 145°F. Remove the lamb from the grill and serve immediately.

Nutrition:

- Calories: 50

- Carbs: 4g

- Fiber: 2g

- Fat: 2.5g

- Protein: 2g

Appetizers and Sides

Grilled Watermelon

Preparation Time: 10 Minutes

Cooking Time: 15 Minutes

Servings: 4

Ingredients:

- 2 Limes

- 2 tbsp. oil

- ½ Watermelon, sliced into wedges

- ¼ tsp. Pepper flakes

- 2 tbsp. Salt

Directions:

1.   Preheat the grill to high with a closed lid.

2.   Brush the watermelon with oil. Grill for 15 minutes. Flip once.

3.   In a blender mix the salt and pepper flakes until combined.

4.   Transfer the watermelon to a plate.

5.   Serve and enjoy!

Nutrition:

- Calories: 40

- Protein: 1g

- Carbs: 10g

- Fat: 0 g

Grilled Mushroom Skewers

Preparation Time: 5 Minutes

Cooking Time: 60 Minutes

Servings: 6

Ingredients:

- 16 - oz. 1 lb. Baby Portobello Mushrooms

For the marinade:

- ¼ cup olive oil

- ¼ cup lemon juice

- Small handful parsley

- 1 tsp. sugar

- 1 tsp. salt

- ¼ tsp. pepper

- ¼ tsp. cayenne pepper

- 1 to 2 garlic cloves

- 1 tbsp. balsamic vinegar

What you will need:

- 10-inch bamboo/wood skewers

Directions:

1. Add the beans to the plate of a lipped container, in an even layer. Shower the softened spread uniformly out ludicrous, and utilizing a couple of tongs tenderly hurl the beans with the margarine until all around covered.

2. Season the beans uniformly, and generously, with salt and pepper.

3. Preheat the smoker to 275°. Include the beans, and smoke 3-4 hours, hurling them like clockwork or until delicate wilted, and marginally seared in spots.

4. Spot 10 medium sticks into a heating dish and spread with water. It's critical to douse the sticks for in any event 15 minutes (more is better) or they will consume too rapidly on the flame broil.

5. Spot the majority of the marinade mixture in a nourishment processor and heartbeat a few times until the marinade is almost smooth.

6. Flush your mushrooms and pat dry. Cut each mushroom down the middle, so each piece has half of the mushroom stem.

7.   Spot the mushroom parts into a big gallon-size Ziploc sack, or a medium bowl and pour in the marinade. Shake the pack until the majority of the mushrooms are equally covered in marinade. Refrigerate and marinate for 30mins to 45mins.

8.   Preheat your barbecue to about 300°F

9.   Stick the mushrooms cozily onto the bamboo/wooden sticks that have been dousing (no compelling reason to dry the sticks). Piercing the mushrooms was a bit irritating from the outset until I got the hang of things.

10.   I've discovered that it's least demanding to stick them by bending them onto the stick. In the event that you simply drive the stick through, it might make the mushroom break.

11.   Spot the pierced mushrooms on the hot barbecue for around 3mins for every side, causing sure the mushrooms don't consume the flame broil. The mushrooms are done when they are delicate; as mushrooms ought to be.

12.   Remove from the barbecue. Spread with foil to keep them warm until prepared to serve

Nutrition:

• Calories: 230

- Carbs: 10g

- Fat: 20g

- Protein: 5g

Bacon Cheddar Slider

Preparation Time: 30 minutes

Cooking Time: 15 minutes

Servings: 6-10 (1-2 sliders each as an appetizer)

Recommended Traeger: Optional

Ingredients:

- 1-pound ground beef (80% lean)

- ½ tsp. garlic salt

- ½ tsp. salt

- ½ tsp. garlic

- ½ tsp. onion

- ½ tsp. black pepper

- 6 bacon slices, cut in half

- ½cup mayonnaise

- 2 tsp. creamy wasabi (optional)

- 6 (1 oz.) sliced sharp cheddar cheese, cut in half (optional)

- Sliced red onion

- ½ cup sliced kosher dill pickles

- 12 mini pieces bread sliced horizontally

- Ketchup

Directions:

1. Place ground beef, garlic salt, seasoned salt, garlic powder, onion powder, and black pepper in a medium bowl.

2. Divide the meat mixture into 12 equal parts, shape into small thin round patties (about 2 ounces each) and save.

3. Cook the bacon on medium heat over medium heat for 5-8 minutes until crunchy. Set aside.

4. To make the sauce, mix the mayonnaise and horseradish in a small bowl.

5. Set up a Traeger smoker grill for direct cooking to use griddle accessories. Contact the manufacturer to see if there is a griddle accessory that works with the wooden Traeger smoker grill.

6. Spray a cooking spray on the griddle cooking surface for best non-stick results.

7. Preheat Traeger smoker grill to 350°F using selected Traegers. The griddle surface should be approximately 400°F.

8. Grill the putty for 3-4 minutes each until the internal temperature reaches 160°F.

9.   If necessary, place a sharp cheddar cheese slice on each patty while the patty is on the griddle or after the patty is removed from the griddle. Place a small amount of mayonnaise mixture, a slice of red onion, and a hamburger pate in the lower half of each roll. Pickled slices, bacon, and ketchup.

Nutrition:

- Calories: 379

- Carbs: 11g

- Protein: 25g

- Fat: 21g

Caprese Tomato Salad

Preparation Time: 5 Minutes

Cooking Time: 60 Minutes

Servings: 4

Ingredients:

- 3 cups halved multicolored cherry tomatoes

- 1/8 tsp. kosher salt

- ½ cup fresh basil leaves

- 1 tbsp. extra-virgin olive oil

- 1 tbsp. balsamic vinegar

- ½ tsp. black pepper

- ¼ tsp. kosher salt

- 1 ounce diced fresh mozzarella cheese (about 1/3 cup)

Directions:

1. Join tomatoes and 1/8 tsp. legitimate salt in a big bowl.

2. Let it rest for 5mins.

3. Include basil leaves, olive oil, balsamic vinegar, pepper, ¼ tsp. fit salt, and mozzarella; toss.

Nutrition:

- Calories: 80

- Fat: 5.8g

- Protein: 2g

- Carb 5g

- Sugars: 4g

Traditional Recipes

Crispy Duck

Preparation Time: 15 minutes

Cooking Time: 4 hours 5 minutes

Servings: 6

Ingredients:

- ¾ cup honey

- ¾ cup soy sauce

- ¾ cup red wine

- 1 tsp. paprika

- 1½ tbsp. garlic salt

- Ground black pepper, as required

- 1 (5-pound) whole duck, giblets removed and trimmed

Directions:

1. Preheat the Traeger grill & Smoker on grill setting to 225-250°F.

2. In a bowl, add all ingredients except for duck and mix until well combined.

3.   With a fork, poke holes in the skin of the duck.

4.   Coat the duck with honey mixture generously.

5.   Arrange duck in traeger gill, breast side down and cook for about 4 hours, coating with honey mixture one after 2 hours.

6.   Remove the duck from grill and place onto a cutting board for about 15 minutes before carving.

7.   With a sharp knife, cut the duck into desired-sized pieces and serve.

Nutrition:

Calories: 878

Fat: 52.1 g

Saturated Fat: 13.9 g

Cholesterol: 3341 mg

Sodium: 2300 mg

Carbs: 45.4 g

Fiber: 0.7 g

Sugar: 39.6 g

Protein: 51 g

Jerked Up Tilapia

Preparation Time: 20 minutes

Cooking Time: 45 minutes

Serving: 8

Ingredients:

- 5 cloves of garlic

- 1 small sized onion

- 3 Jalapeno Chiles

- 3 tsp. of ground ginger

- 3 tbsp. of light brown Sugar:

- 3 tsp. of dried thyme

- 2 tsp. of salt

- 2 tsp. of ground cinnamon

- 1 tsp. of black pepper

- 1 tsp. of ground allspice

- ¼ tsp. of cayenne pepper

- 4 -6 ounce of tilapia fillets

- ¼ cup of olive oil

- 1 cup of sliced up carrots

- 1 bunch of whole green onions

- 2 tbsp. of whole allspice

Directions:

1.   Take a blending bowl and combine the first 11 of the listed ingredients and puree them nicely using your blender or food processor

2.   Add the fish pieces in a large-sized zip bag and toss in the pureed mixture alongside olive oil

3.   Seal it up and press to make sure that the fish is coated well

4.   Let it marinate in your fridge for at least 30 minutes to 1 hour

5.   Take your drip pan and add water, cover with aluminum foil. Pre-heat your smoker to 225°F

6.   Use water fill water pan halfway through and place it over drip pan. Add wood chips to the side tray

7.   Take a medium-sized bowl and toss in some pecan wood chips and soak them underwater alongside whole allspice

8.   Prepare an excellent 9x 13-inch foil pan by poking a dozen holes and spraying it with non-stick cooking spray

9.   Spread out the carrots, green onions across the bottom of the pan

10.   Arrange the fishes on top of them

11.   Place the container in your smoker

12.   Smoke for about 45 minutes making sure to add more chips after every 15 minutes until the internal temperature of the fish rises to 145°Fahrenheit

13.   Serve hot

Nutrition:

- Calories: 347

- Fats: 19g

- Carbs: 18g

- Fiber: 1g

CPSIA information can be obtained
at www.ICGtesting.com
Printed in the USA
BVHW061813240321
603332BV00007B/994

9 781801 942355